# Insect's Body

**Jean Feldman and Holly Karapetkova**

*Tune: Head, Shoulders, Knees, and Toes*

ROURKE CLASSROOM

www.rourkeclassroom.com

Head, thorax, abdomen – abdomen!

Head, thorax, abdomen – abdomen!

And eyes

And mouth

And antennae, two

Six legs

And there's an insect for you!

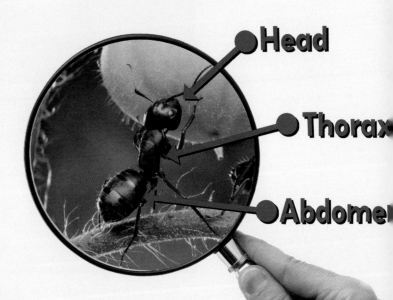

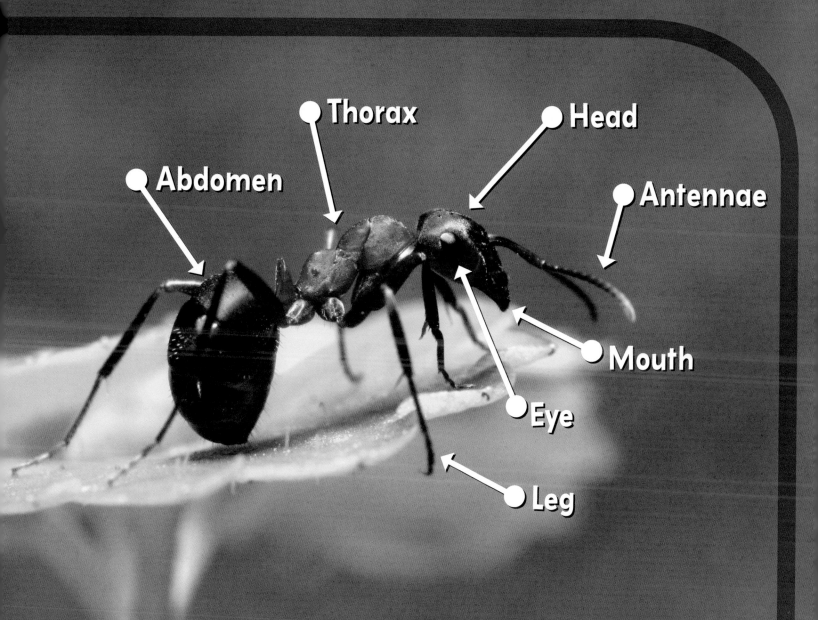

*Hmmm,* thorax, abdomen – abdomen!

*Hmmm,* thorax, abdomen – abdomen!

And eyes

And mouth

And antennae, two

Six legs

And there's an insect for you!

Head

*Hmmm, hmmmmm,* **abdomen – abdomen!**

*Hmmm, hmmmmm,* **abdomen – abdomen!**

And eyes

And mouth

And antennae, two

Six legs

And there's an insect for you!

Thorax

*Hmmm, hmmmmm, hmmmmmm – hmmmmmm!*

*Hmmm, hmmmmm, hmmmmmm – hmmmmmm!*

And eyes

And mouth

And antennae, two

Six legs

And there's an insect for you!

Abdomen

Abdomen

*Hmmm, hmmmmm, hmmmmmm – hmmmmmm!*

*Hmmm, hmmmmm, hmmmmmm – hmmmmmm!*

*Hmm hmmm*

And mouth

And antennae, two

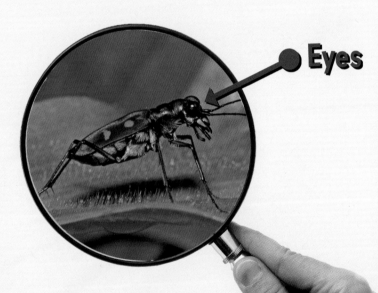

Eyes

Six legs

And there's an insect for you!

*Hmmm, hmmmmm, hmmmmm – hmmmmm!*

*Hmmm, hmmmmm, hmmmmm – hmmmmm!*

*Hmm hmmm*

*Hmm hmmmm*

And antennae, two

Six legs

And there's an insect for you!

**Mouth**

Hmmm, hmmmmm, hmmmmmm – hmmmmm!

Hmmm, hmmmmm, hmmmmmm – hmmmmm!

Hmm hmmm

Hmm hmmmm

Hmm hmmmmmmm, hmm

Six legs

And there's an insect for you!

**Antennae**

Antennae

Hmmm, hmmmmm, hmmmmmm – hmmmmmm!

Hmmm, hmmmmm, hmmmmmm – hmmmmmm!

Hmm hmmm

Hmm hmmmm

Hmm hmmmmmmm, hmm

Hmm hmmm

**And there's an insect for you!**

Legs